Freda Lewis-Hall, M.D.

Make your Mark!

WHY LEGACY STILL MATTERS

Published by The Healthcare Businesswomen's Association

Cover Design: Cindy Luu of CluuDesign
Cover Photo: John Halpern
Interior Design: Page Grafx, Inc.

Library of Congress Cataloging in Publication Data
Lewis-Hall, Freda
Make your mark! Why legacy still matters/ Freda Lewis-Hall, M.D.

ISBN: 978-0-9884946-0-2
Library of Congress Control Number: 2012952868

To my beloved mother and father, who told me I could fly and gave me wings. You are why I soar.

To Randy, my husband and heartthrob, my cheerleader on the days when I thought I could and my rock on the days I was convinced I could not. You are why I stand.

To our children, Erin, Justin and Austin, who have brought us profound pride and great joy. You are why I strive.

To my family, friends and colleagues—you have stood by my side and always had my back. You are why I share.

To patients everywhere, especially those awaiting new cures. You are why I serve.

Acknowledgments

This is the first time I've written about the lessons of my life, but I'm sure it won't be my last as I am not a "one and done" person. However, I now better understand what writing and publishing are all about—notably, that it's a team effort. I want to thank my family and friends who worked with me on this project and who kept my eyes on the prize.

First, I want to thank John Santoro, my colleague and collaborator on this project. John is a passionate advocate for the patients all of us at Pfizer are pledged to serve. This story would not have been written without his deep knowledge and skill, as well as his faith in me.

I also want to thank Ian Read, Pfizer's Chairman and CEO, my colleagues on the Executive Leadership Team, and my colleagues in Pfizer Medical for their support of this effort. I am so proud to be engaged in our company's most vital work.

The Healthcare Businesswomen's Association is my partner on this book. It is also one of the world's most important and impactful professional organizations. I want to thank Laurie Cooke, Yvonne D'Amelio, Eve Dryer, Buket Grau, Nora Leary, Carol Meerschaert, Charlotte Sibley and Wendy White for their hard work in helping me in framing and publishing my thinking.

I am thankful for all the people I have been fortunate to know and rely on during my career, and I am greatly encouraged by the talent and dedication of the next generation. I hope that this work will help leaders everywhere understand both the responsibility of leadership and the importance of legacy, even in this blazing-fast world.

Contents

Foreword

Why Legacy Must Matter

This publication is based on a speech titled "Turning *Us* Around: Lessons from a Life in Patient Care." It's a speech I gave in May 2011 when I was honored to be named as "Woman of the Year" by the Healthcare Businesswomen's Association. My talk covered a series of topics, including the need for a top-to-bottom reappraisal of how we in healthcare view ourselves, given the nagging lack of trust by the public in what we do. On a personal level, my talk centered on legacy, and why it is more important than ever, even in a world where memories are short and fame is fleeting.

I appreciate that, for many leaders, thinking about legacy usually takes a back seat to the crises of the moment. Yet I firmly believe that leadership and legacy are inextricably entwined. The leaders with the greatest influence on our lives not only take their legacies seriously, but also begin early on to shape them. Memorable leaders look to profoundly change a corner of the world and pass the baton of leadership to a network of people whom they have inspired. In that way, leaders never die, or even fade away. Their influence is transformed into insights and memories carried forward and put to use by the next generation.

I offer this publication for people who consider themselves leaders or who are readying themselves for leadership. The key lesson of this book is simply stated: take your legacy seriously, now. This lesson is anchored in the experiences of my life, as well as those of the people who shaped me.

It is only fitting that this work should be published in partnership with the Healthcare Businesswomen's Association, whose mission is to help women at all levels attain their aspirations in one of the world's most noble professions. Whatever you do, whomever you lead, however you envision your legacy, I believe that what you read here will help you recognize that your contributions are important, that your legacy genuinely matters, and that the time to forge your legacy begins *right now*!

Freda Lewis-Hall, M.D.

Chapter 1

The Essential Questions of Legacy

How Do You Think About Legacy?

For many years I've been thinking about legacy—and by "many years" I mean nearly my entire life. I was an only child, and by most eyewitness accounts, an unusual one. I was introverted and cerebral, and spent a lot of time thinking about my future. By age six, inspired by our family physician, Dr. William Settles, I knew what I wanted to be in life. A few years after that, my late mother, Jeanette Lewis, helped me "turn myself around"—to be true to myself but sensitive to the impression I left on people around me. Soon after that I became keenly curious about the concept of one's legacy—and especially concerned about mine.

If the idea of a kid thinking about legacy seems strange, you have to remember the tenor of the times when I was coming of age. This was the 1960s, a decade of tremendous political change and cataclysmic social upheaval. For African-Americans, the decade lurched wildly between hope and horror. It seemed every time my parents turned on the evening news, the talk was of legacy—including the legacies of leaders such as Malcolm X, John and Bobby Kennedy, and the Rev. Martin Luther King, Jr., all of whom should have had decades of leadership before them.

Sometime during the turmoil of the late 1960s, I turned to my wise father, Harvey Lewis, whom I revered (and still do), and asked him a question that probably wasn't on the minds of most teenagers.

"Daddy ... What do you think my legacy will be?"

Daddy was surprised that I asked such a question, but he was also quick to answer it.

FREDA LEWIS-HALL

Graduation from Johns Hopkins, 1976. Both my parents understood the importance of education and sacrificed greatly to support mine. They also understood the strong connection between leadership and legacy.

The Call of Duty

While Daddy couldn't know then what my legacy would be, he did offer a way to measure it. He said it would be the sum of:

- What I leave behind
- Who I bring behind
- What I learn along the way

Having grown up under difficult circumstances in the segregated South, both my parents had the wisdom to answer just about any of life's questions. When it came to my question about legacy, though, it was my father who offered this memorable answer, drawing on his extraordinary life experiences.

"Develop Your Balance for the Curves— Not for the Straightaways"

Born in Richmond, Virginia, Harvey Lewis grew up in a large family where he learned both self-reliance and the importance of familial support. Love held the family together through the Depression when work and money just disappeared. During World War II, my father, along with four of his brothers, enlisted in the Army knowing full well the harsh discrimination many minorities faced in the then-segregated Armed Forces. The Lewis brothers and thousands of other minority Americans were being asked by their country to risk their lives to turn back fascism—and then return to "back of the bus" citizenship.

Ever loyal to his country, my father did his duty and, after the war, took a job as a Pullman porter. He joined the legion of African-Americans who served passengers in railroad sleeping cars in the days before air travel became both affordable and convenient. It was an interesting job that brought him face-to-face with America's rich and powerful, and gave him an opportunity to see sights most young men his age and race could not envision. It was also a difficult job, right at the front lines of racial discrimination. Injustice ran rampant. In the late 1940s and early 1950s, because of their color, my parents were barred from buying tickets in the first-class compartments where my father worked. At some of the whistle stops along his routes, the fountains, public bathrooms and restaurants were labeled "White" and "Colored."

Daddy took all of this in stride. Reflecting on the era, my father would echo the advice given him by veteran porters on keeping his footing while the train moved at high speed. "Develop your balance for the curves," they told him. "Then the straightaways will take care of themselves."

Driving Washington

My father's life took a number of curves. He married his love, my mother Jeanette, and they took up life in Washington, D.C., running the dry cleaning service on an Army base. That alone didn't pay all the bills, so he also took a job as a taxi driver. Again, he saw all dimensions of life, brushing up against some of the most influential people in the nation's capital while managing to make it from paycheck to paycheck.

Given his life experience, it's no surprise that my father became active in the 1960s movement for equality and civil rights. One of my earliest memories was his involvement in the August 1963 March on Washington that propelled Rev. Martin Luther King, Jr. to national prominence. Daddy drove his van to the March, picking up people, usually total strangers, who needed a ride to the National Mall. He was early (as usual) to the event, so he scored a prime seat close to the podium, where he heard Rev. King's now-famous "I Have a Dream" call for justice and equality.

I also remember the backlash three weeks later—the horrifying bombing of an African-American congregation in Birmingham, Alabama. Four black girls were killed as they prayed in church. Two months later came my first "What were you doing when you heard the news?" moment—the assassination of President John F. Kennedy.

I remember my father making endless trips to shuttle mourners to the Capitol Rotunda, where President Kennedy's body lay in state. He was also working in Washington through the terrifying days of April 1968 when the city exploded in flames after the assassination of Rev. King. After the second day of riots, my mother put her foot down and insisted that Daddy stay home. Driving in D.C. was just too perilous.

Given the wrenching waves of change my father witnessed in 20th century America, it is not surprising that he had a ready answer to my question about defining a legacy.

What you leave behind … who you bring behind … and what you learn along the way: I'll call these the three "pressure tests" of legacy, and in the chapters that unfold, discuss why they are important to us as leaders.

CLAIRE ALLISON PHOTOGRAPHY

My father and I celebrate my 2011 Woman of the Year Award from the Healthcare Businesswomen's Association. His advice on legacy is the cornerstone of this book— and my life.

Building a Sense of Urgency:
"We're Finding You a College. Starting Tonight."

While just thinking about your legacy is a good start, the earlier you can begin shaping it, the better. In my case, I knew that I wanted a career in medicine and began to think about college while in high school in Annapolis, Maryland—home of the U.S. Naval Academy. Early in my senior year, I visited with my guidance counselor to discuss my plans for the future. My head swam with questions about college and beyond, but as I began to ask them, the counselor gently cut me off and said:

> **"Miss Lewis, you're a nice young lady. You're smart and you're attractive. Instead of college, why don't you think about marrying a Midshipman? You'd make a wonderful officer's wife!"**

That was the end of discussion. I left her office and made my way home, baffled by the conversation and wondering what my years of academic accomplishment had won for me. Getting married—that was it for me? That was all I could offer? I had nothing against the Navy, against the Naval Academy, or against being married. I just thought I could forge my own destiny, and it was painful to hear otherwise, no matter how misguided the opinion.

Later, at home, my mother, who faithfully encouraged me in all my endeavors, sensed my anxiety. She asked me to talk about what was bothering me, and I did, laying out the whole story. She listened quietly with her lips pursed and then said, firmly, "We're finding you a college. Starting tonight."

We drove over to the local drug store and bought all the latest guides to the nation's best colleges. For most of that night, we read out loud to each other and talked about my future. Later that week, we began applying to colleges, starting with Number 1 on the list, shooting out applications to places like Harvard, Princeton, Brown and Johns Hopkins, and keeping it up until the application money ran out.

I was accepted at a number of the top schools, but chose Hopkins, mostly because of its reputation for medicine. In the fall of 1972, I set off for my freshman year in my first car: a refurbished, repainted taxi, thanks to my father. I was secure in my vision of becoming a doctor, and excited about the legacy I could build from there.

Soon, however, I had serious misgivings about my choice of schools. Johns Hopkins was 40 miles from my home, but it may as well have been on a different planet.

Hopkins had just a handful of African-Americans in its student body and no African-American professors. While most students treated us well, a surprising number of them, and even some professors, had no reservations about expressing hostility toward the new kids on campus. I finished in three years, in part because I felt I never fit in at school.

Today I've come to terms with my college experience and see the good my Hopkins education did for me. I also know that things have changed immensely there since the "Golden Decade" of the 1970s, when African-Americans enrolled in significant numbers in top colleges around America. I'm reminded by my husband and fellow Hopkins graduate, Randy Hall, that we were among the pioneers who changed some of America's most elite institutions. That may be true, but it doesn't alter the reality: pioneers often feel cold and lonely, and a lot of them become discouraged and don't finish the trail. It took me ten years after graduating to work up the courage to set foot again on the Hopkins campus. From all this I learned a valuable life-lesson— **a sincere welcome goes a long way to positively shaping your perceptions and feelings about a major life event like college or a new career.**

Staying the Course

Having completed my undergraduate studies in three years, I planned to use what would have been my senior year to earn the money I'd need for medical school. I went to work in D.C. for the

Federal Power Commission, which also employed my father at the time. I lived at home, saved my paychecks, and continued planning my options.

Nightly discussions around the dinner table often centered on my plans for medical school. I worked nearly in the shadow of the school I had in mind: Howard University College of Medicine. I put in an application and waited.

My mother, in her ever-wise ways, kept telling me to "just go down to Howard and see if they'll put you in their medical school." I explained that medical schools didn't work that way, but then figured I'd head over to Howard and follow up on my application. One day, on my lunch hour, I hustled over to the medical college and was fortunate to meet an admission staffer who went well "beyond the call" when it came to helping me. She took me aside and said, "We're doing interviews today and just had a slot open up. Are you game?"

I called my office, asked my colleagues to cover for me at work, and plunged cold into a formal interview for a place at Howard University College of Medicine. It was one of my earliest lessons in leadership. **When opportunity calls, don't wait for the second ring.**

A few weeks later, after scads of prayers, dozens of follow-up calls, and favorable marks on the MCATs, I received the welcome "thick envelope" notice that I was accepted into the class of 1980. I didn't yet have a legacy, but through some very fortuitous events and quick decisions, I had created a future.

Fast Forward

Late in 2010, nearly 30 years after medical school, I was asked by one of my Pfizer colleagues, Dr. Toni Hoover, for permission to float my name as a candidate for Woman of the Year from the HBA—the Healthcare Businesswomen's Association.

Of all my professional affiliations, I value the HBA among the highest, and I know many of the previous "WOTY" awardees. They are among the most prominent women in healthcare.

HBA

One of the proudest and
most nerve-wracking days
of my life—HBA Woman
of the Year Luncheon,
New York City, May 2011.

I told Toni I thought it was the longest of long shots but if she
wanted to start the ball rolling, I would certainly be honored. The rolling ball became an avalanche of support from friends and colleagues
throughout healthcare, and I was soon thrilled to learn that I would be
the 2011 HBA Woman of the Year.

The award ceremony would take place at the annual HBA Woman
of the Year luncheon in May. I would be "crowned," so to speak, in
front of 2,500 HBA members, guests and media—most of them gath-
ered at the New York Hilton, others watching live in San Francisco and
Paris. I was expected to make a speech—not a ceremonial speech, not
a couple of quick quips, but a meaty presentation on a topic of intense
interest—say, the future of healthcare.

I'm no stranger to public speaking, but this speech had me on
edge. Over the months leading up to the event, I worked with my team
crafting draft after draft. Nothing seemed to fit "just right." It wasn't

until the day before the luncheon that I felt truly comfortable with my written remarks.

At the appointed hour, people poured into the ballroom—thousands of them, elbow to elbow. The luncheon itself was a blur of accolades. There were touching speeches by HBA executives and the outgoing Woman of the Year; shout-outs to dozens of HBA "Rising Stars" and a spirited introduction by my boss, Pfizer's Chief Executive Officer, Ian Read. In the front row sat my then 92-year-old father, Harvey Lewis, my husband Randy, our kids, and the rest of my family, all beaming with pride. I felt my mother's presence deep in my heart. Tears of joy, and those of deep longing, welled in my eyes.

Suddenly, Ian was wrapping up, and I was in the spotlight, feeling awfully alone.

I began to speak, to thank my loved ones, and to launch into my thinking on leadership and legacy. I used some of my prepared remarks, but whatever came out of my mouth over the next 15 minutes bore only a passing resemblance to the speech loaded into the teleprompter.

All I know is that people responded. There were tears when I spoke about my mother; laughter when I talked about bringing up the kids; and a long, loud, standing ovation when I finished with the three "pressure tests" of legacy my father had given to me:

- What you leave behind
- Who you bring behind
- What you learn along the way

The audience applauded wildly after my speech, but to this day, I can't remember how I got through it.

At the reception afterwards, I fielded dozens of questions from young HBA members—could I tell them more about my parents' vision of legacy and leadership?

More important, could I tell them how to put this vision into practice? Could I talk more about why legacy was so important in a world where everyone gets 15 minutes of fame?

Sure I could. Grab a chair and sit back. Here goes.

Chapter 2

What You Leave Behind

A Framework for Legacy

My father's first "pressure test" of legacy is "what we leave behind." Unlike the pharaohs, we can't leave behind pyramids. What we *can* leave behind is:

- A profoundly changed corner of the world and/or
- A network of the inspired

Whatever your legacy, whatever you leave behind, it all begins with a compelling vision for leadership, with emphasis on "compelling." That point was made crystal clear to me in 2011 when I had the opportunity to meet Dr. A. P. J. Abdul Kalam, the president of India from 2002 to 2007. A scientist, poet, philosopher and statesman, Dr. Kalam is revered in his country as a leader who helped propel India toward greater leadership in technology. In a talk he gave in New York in 2011, he stressed that profound change begins with a vision so compelling that it should never let you rest.

Two Women, Two Paths, One Vision, No Sleep

A compelling vision can certainly orient an entire career. In thinking about people who relentlessly pursued their leadership visions, and profoundly changed their corners of the world, I often focus on two inspiring women who were impassioned activists for better healthcare—Alice F. Oliver and Carolyn Buck Luce. Both achieved senior leadership positions in great organizations; both took entirely different paths to their pinnacle positions; and both remind us that whatever our vision may be, it should—in the words of Dr. Kalam— never let us rest.

Alice F. Oliver

A one-sentence summary of Alice's career might read something like "a long-time executive with pharmaceutical company Eli Lilly." That phrase does little justice to her prodigious body of work. An African-American raised in the small towns of Alabama and Tennessee, Alice joined Lilly in 1968 as a member of the clerical pool, working full-time by day while she finished college at night. She earned her degree in psychology from Butler University in 1970 and applied for an entry-level professional job with Lilly in what was then called "Personnel," now Human Resources. Alice was told her psychology degree did not qualify her for the job she wanted, and that Lilly preferred candidates with stronger indications of management potential.

Undaunted, Alice petitioned Lilly to move her to an evening job so she could continue toward her goal of earning a master's degree, which would qualify her to be an employee counselor or coach. Typists weren't needed in the evening, so Alice asked to join the office cleaning staff.

Her managers at Lilly were at first reluctant to approve the move, afraid that they'd be accused of deliberately demoting a black woman into a janitor's job. Eventually they relented. Alice cleaned offices for nearly three years, earned her master's in social work from Indiana University and, in 1975, was hired into the professional entry-level ranks at Lilly. After assignments in the Elizabeth Arden beauty products and medical divisions, she took on her first professional HR role in 1980, a decade after she first set her sights on it.

By 1983, Alice had her first mid-level management position. In 1989, she became a director, emerging as one of the pioneers who brought HR off the sidelines and into partnership with leaders of a business. She did this not only by being an outstanding HR professional but also by understanding how HR could add value to business decisions and the business as a whole. Alice understood the leverage points of a business, its competitive landscape, and its strengths and weaknesses. Numbers never intimidated her. Asked how she navigated business so readily without an M.B.A., she said that her life experiences had taught her all she needed to know to survive in a competitive environment. "Nothing corporate America could throw at me could surpass what I saw and experienced growing up in the Deep South," she said. "My survival instincts became fully developed because of those experiences. I was ready for anything."

Her life experiences also led her to success in a challenging arena—coaching high-potential executives on their leadership and communications skills. She had a reputation for delivering dead-honest feedback but doing so in ways that encouraged change in even the most prickly of corporate leaders.

I had the good fortune to meet Alice at Lilly and have her as one of my first executive coaches. Her advice was simple and elegant. "Know yourself better than anyone else can," she told me. "Know your strengths—they will carry you forward. Know your weaknesses—acknowledge them and work on them to minimize their hold on you and their effects on your career. Then you won't worry about them so much and obsess about them being used against you."

She had special counsel for me, an African-American woman making the jump from academia to corporate life. "No matter what you encounter, never, ever allow yourself to think as a victim. That only saps your energy and gives you excuses."

Alice became one of Lilly's most respected professionals, eventually becoming the head of HR for a Lilly division. She was instrumental in forging Lilly's diversity strategy and served as an ambassador for the company, speaking frequently to college students on life in the corporate world. Then, following her retirement in 1999, Alice faced an unthinkable personal tragedy, the sudden death of her daughter from an unknown medical cause. "Every obstacle, every challenge in my career had its intended purpose," she said, "to help me overcome the worst that life could bring."

Clearly, Alice was no overnight success. But she was a success nevertheless, thanks to her vision, dedication and willingness to analyze her situation candidly and realistically. She profoundly changed a corner of the world in her profession and her company. And she left behind a network of people like me, who to this day are inspired by her persistence, resilience and relentless optimism.

Carolyn Buck Luce

While Alice F. Oliver spent her entire career with Lilly, Carolyn Buck Luce, one of my other role models, made her way to prominence by excelling in a number of disciplines and becoming a leader in several organizations. Carolyn has a unique approach to career planning—she believes in planning her life in 10-year segments, largely

Carolyn Buck Luce, head of Ernst & Young's Global Life Sciences Practice. Carolyn's amazing body of work covers diplomacy, finance, business, entrepreneurship, and advocacy for women.

HBA/CAROLYN BUCK LUCE

re-inventing herself every decade. Not only is she one of the leading thinkers about the future of healthcare, she's also an agent of change for the advancement of women and girls, constantly questioning why the world's women remain, in her words, "under-served, under-appreciated, and under-utilized."

Carolyn has scary brainpower. If intelligence could light cities, she'd illuminate Las Vegas. She mastered Russian in college, graduated Phi Beta Kappa from Georgetown University, and was accepted into the Foreign Service, going to work overseas for the U.S. Information Agency (USIA). She was posted to Moscow in an entry-level job that certainly must have set her thinking about the under-utilization of women.

While she saw men with nowhere near her smarts and skills getting coveted analyst positions, Carolyn's first assignment was to work in a USIA-sponsored model of a "typical" American home, talking with residents of the Soviet Union about life in the United States.

The teachable moment here is that Carolyn's exhibit and the others that the USIA offered over the years were surprisingly effective. Carolyn and her colleagues could talk candidly—in fluent Russian—about life and culture in America. They didn't describe the U.S.A. as Utopia but openly addressed the average Russian citizen's perceptions of America—good and bad. In so doing, they put a human face on a Cold War opponent. According to Carolyn, the USIA exhibits resonated most soundly with the growing numbers of well-educated Russians, some of whom were later instrumental in dismantling the Soviet empire.

For the next 10-year chapter of her life, Carolyn returned to the U.S.A., earned an M.B.A. from Columbia, and put her knowledge of international relations to work for Citibank. There she learned about the formidable power of information and technology, as Citi was in the vanguard of reshaping banking through technology, including the widespread use of ATMs.

After attracting the attention of Wall Street, Carolyn moved to investment banking. She then became an entrepreneur, starting her own broker/dealer banking firm before joining accounting giant Ernst & Young as a consultant, where she volunteered to help build the firm's global pharmaceutical practice.

Her passion for healthcare was further enhanced by her marriage in 1992 to Rev. Forrest Church, the long-time pastor of the Unitarian Church of All Souls on Manhattan's Upper East Side. On February 2, 2008, Rev. Church announced to his congregation that he had advanced esophageal cancer and was entering the last stages of his life's journey. His sermon that day, titled "Love and Death," should be required reading for all of us in patient care. In it, he addressed Carolyn and all caregivers on the support needed in approaching the final passage.

> **"The act of releasing a loved one from all further obligations as he lies dying—to tell him it's all right, that he is safe, that we love him and he can go now—is life's most perfect gift, the final expression of unconditional love. We let go for dear life."**

Rev. Church died on September 24, 2009.

I believe Carolyn's passion for healthcare is rooted in her experience as a caregiver, both to her husband and to her four children. She often talks about being a role model for her children, giving them, in her words, "guidance on how to live a life worth dying for."

"You Have to Build Your Network *Before* You Need It."

Much of Carolyn's legacy centers on enlightening people about how women advance in the workforce, and, conversely, what holds women back. She was one of the co-founders of the Hidden Brain Drain Task Force, a consortium of organizations working on second-generation policies and practices to move more women toward senior leadership. She is also a driving force for gender equity and women's advancement at Ernst & Young. A strong believer in the power of networking,

Carolyn counsels women to build a network before it is needed, just as one should fix a hole in the roof while the sun is shining.

Carolyn once asked me to participate in Ernst & Young's annual "Issues on My Mind" program, bringing together about 200 executive women from client organizations for a day of candid dialogue. The talk quickly turned to the uncomfortable relationship most women have with power. Carolyn says, "Power is not a dirty word. It comes from your knowledge, position, relationships, brand, and personality. And it can, and should, be used constuctively on *behalf* of others, rather than *over* others."

I remember telling the audience that from my perspective, I only wished the glass ceiling was in fact made of glass. To me, it seemed like concrete, with a lead lining to boot. It took me a long time to understand that for all our belief in the mythology about the best people rising naturally to leadership, we all face overt and unconscious biases that have to be accounted for—and overcome—if we are to ultimately demolish the glass ceiling for the next generation.

Carolyn Buck Luce's legacy is already well established, but I am convinced that her best work lies ahead. She, too, is a "Woman of the Year" of the Healthcare Businesswomen's Association, and a wonderful role model for women—and men—everywhere.

A Network of the Inspired

Like Alice and Carolyn, we all can aspire to profoundly change a corner of the world. We can also aspire to make our legacies timeless—to leave behind a network of people inspired by our leadership and achievements. The events of one workday in the spring of 2012 brought home that message to me.

It was the day we hosted what we call "Grand Rounds" at Pfizer—when we assemble our medical community to learn from an outside expert. That expert was Roni Zeiger, a physician who served as Google's chief health officer and now, with Gilles Frydman, runs a start-up cleverly named "Impatient Science." The day was memora-

ble not only in what we learned, but also in showing us that our legacies of leadership can build widespread, connected "networks of the
inspired."

I first met Roni at TEDMED, the annual ideafest that is an offshoot
of the well-known TED conferences. TED—which stands for Technology, Entertainment and Design—started in 1984 as a conference
designed to bring together experts from these then-disparate worlds.
Since then, TED has grown to become a leading forum for exchanging
and developing ideas. TEDMED extends this approach to healthcare
and medicine, and has evolved into a community of leaders passionate about creating a better future for healthcare.

TEDMED is chaired by Jay Walker, a bundle of energy, creativity,
charisma, and humor. A few hours with Jay will leave you breathless.
He is, as the saying goes, "focused on everything."

In 2011, Jay invited me to be active in TEDMED and to speak at its
showcase event. I was grouped in a flight of six speakers that included
three corporate chief medical officers, architect Michael Graves, ma-
gician Eric Mead and singer-songwriter Loudon Wainwright III.

Now there's a parlay for you!

My talk was a call to action on the concept of "metacollaboration"—transcending the boundaries that separate us in pursuit of a
goal that none of us, on our own, can achieve. This is not a new concept
but it has some interesting new applications. In my TEDMED talk, I
spoke about polio and how it affected my family, and how a coalition
of universities, pharmaceutical companies, government agencies and
a grassroots movement called the March of Dimes developed and put
into widespread use Dr. Jonas Salk's polio vaccine. These groups
didn't always have a lot of love for each other, but they were able
to find common ground—defeating a dreaded disease. Without the
foresight of these diverse groups to overcome their differences and
collaborate at new levels of effectiveness, we might still be using iron
lungs.

At TEDMED, I called for a kick-start on a metacollaboration to
turn back the fast-rising tide of Alzheimer's—and began soliciting

meta-collaboration (n) 1. master collaboration that productively links disparate knowledge and assets to problem-solve in every dimension and accelerate solutions 2. a seamless innovation ecosystem

PFIZER

Speaking at TEDMED, one of the world's premier
spaces for collaboration and idea sharing. My talk can
be viewed on YouTube (http://bit.ly/rwvt17).

ideas for an approach that would engage the world's many Alzheimer's
groups to share more of their knowledge. Within a few days of my talk,
more than 200 people had expressed interest in participating, and a
network of the inspired began to take shape.

The speech seemed to be well received, at least from the "tweets"
being sent live from the ballroom, and after I finished, I was told that
an admirer was waiting for me in the wings. That was Roni, then with
Google. We spoke of his team's work in predicting the incidence of
infectious diseases by tracking the patterns of search terms. Graph
out the reports on flu cases by the Centers for Disease Control and
Prevention, overlay the numbers of people who search "flu symp-
toms" on the Web, and the correlation is nearly perfect. Roni's work is

reshaping the way authorities track common communicable diseases. Type "Google Flu Trends" into your browser and you can check this for yourself, and see how your state and maybe even your city are doing in terms of flu prevalence.

Inspired by his brilliance and enthusiasm, I invited Roni to speak at Pfizer, and by the time he was able to accept, he had left Google and founded Impatient Science.

Roni talked to us about the need for more feedback loops from "bedside to bench" so that doctors and drug researchers could learn more from what he called "the expert patient." He has a vision where entire networks of patients who share a disease or symptom can be more closely connected with the doctors specializing in that disease or advancing research on it. It was an intriguing and highly provocative idea, and I wanted to know more about it.

One of the Good Guys

Roni and I continued the conversation over lunch outside our cafeteria, and there we were introduced to a physician at Pfizer who spoke about his previous experience with Merck. I smiled and said, "I'm one of the Good Guys!"—and it was immediately evident who I knew at Merck, and why.

The Good Guys is a virtual organization that focuses on spreading the word about early detection of prostate cancer. It was founded by Dr. Richard "Buzz" Goodstein, a physician whose body of work and efforts to form a network of the inspired continue to shape the fight against prostate cancer today.

Buzz pioneered remote learning for continuing medical education (CME) as the writer, producer and on-camera talent for a CME TV series called *Mind and Body*, which was later picked up by PBS. After being recruited to Merck, he became an early adopter of the Internet, creating much of the material that became the forerunner of WebMD, and later set the stage for groups such as Google Health and, yes, Impatient Science.

And thus, the circle is unbroken.

Late in the 1990s, Buzz moved from Merck to Bayer, where he established a clinical science division and founded the Bayer Institute for Healthcare Communications, a fully not-for-profit foundation that earned accreditation for the continuing education of healthcare professionals.

Buzz retired in 2006 and was diagnosed with advanced prostate cancer that same year. He then created an Internet-based working group—the Good Guys—dedicated to advancing information on prostate cancer. He devoted his final years to this group, and also traveled the nation teaching organizational leaders about prostate cancer. His blogs, e-mails and presentations were legendary, and his influence helped change the way men are tested for prostate cancer. No longer is just reading the PSA number enough. Doctors today also must determine the velocity of change in PSA numbers, a change that Buzz advocated and one that has led to earlier cancer detection and many saved lives.

Buzz died in November 2009. His Good Guys network lives on and now encompasses those who knew Buzz as well as those who never met him. The Good Guys are now hundreds of men and women—a genuine "network of the inspired" that will continue to follow Buzz's memorable counsel—**Think, Feel, Respond, and Pay Forward.**

"What Doesn't Kill Us …"

Prostate cancer, which inspired Buzz Goodstein to build his networks to advance earlier detection, also inspired another important network of collaborators—FasterCures, the Milken Institute's center devoted to speeding the pace of biomedical solutions. FasterCures, like the Milken Institute itself, was founded by Michael Milken, the entrepreneur whose fight with prostate cancer led him to focus his brainpower and the force of his personality on removing the roadblocks that stymie biomedical research.

It's hard to overestimate Michael Milken's influence on prostate cancer and its ripple effects to the treatment of other cancers and other disease areas. In 1993, the year that prostate cancer nearly killed Michael, an estimated 35,000 men died from the disease. Few men had routine diagnostic tests, and fewer still understood the importance of knowing their PSA numbers. That year, Michael went on an unprecedented drive against prostate cancer, envisioning (and backing with funding) a highly focused campaign to raise awareness and speed up the flow of new treatments. Along the way, he became an expert on both the biology of prostate cancer and on the long, labored process of clinical testing and new product approval. Many opinion leaders at the time dismissed him as well-meaning but naïve. Michael, thankfully, proved them wrong. In the span of a decade, diagnostic tests for prostate cancer have become more routine, funding for new therapies has increased, and a range of new therapies have begun to take hold. Two decades after Michael's bout with the disease, the number of U.S. deaths from prostate cancer has fallen by 20 percent, despite an overall rise in the nation's population and a huge rise in the number of older men. I'd argue that Michael Milken was a lever behind much of this remarkable progress.

Michael's influence is possibly best seen in the healthcare retreats he sponsors, which often bring together the nation's top thinkers on healthcare policy, along with research luminaries and patient advocates. An amazing spectrum of personalities, all of them with a personal bond with Michael, gathers at these retreats. What's most impressive is that Michael never allows these gatherings to be talk for talk's sake. Instead, his "network of the inspired" conceives and activates new ways to streamline the drug discovery and development process and to speed the creation and adoption of new "precision medicine" approaches, based on advances in science and technology that can help us learn how to use different treatments in different people for the best possible outcomes.

What Are You Leaving Behind?

Whatever you choose to leave behind—a network of the inspired, a profoundly changed corner of the world, or both—take heart in the lessons of the individuals featured in this chapter. I've tried to acquaint you with a variety of people and their unique situations. The takeaway is this: you need not be rich, powerful or famous to make a measurable difference in the success of your organization, or in the lives of others. However, you *do* need a compelling vision, a willingness to take a leap of faith in your ability, and a core belief in the importance of what you leave behind for others to build upon.

Chapter 3

Who You Bring Behind

My father's second "pressure test" of legacy is "who you bring behind." More to the point, he recognized the "multiplier effect" of the people you help develop and bring forward to leadership.

I came to understand the power of this "multiplier effect" early in my life, through one of my father's 15 siblings, my Uncle C. He contracted polio in 1925, at age 6. While polio was often a mild disease, in about one in 100 cases, the virus viciously attacked and destroyed nerves. Such was the case with Uncle C. Doctors did not expect him to live a year, but he survived for many more, although he remained paralyzed from the waist down for the rest of his life.

My father and the rest of our family were living in Richmond, Virginia, at the time of Uncle C.'s illness, and when it became apparent that his paralysis would be permanent, the Lewises faced an awful situation. They were already poor and the country was entering the Depression, when things would get much worse. They were descendents of slaves living in the former capital of the Confederacy, and they were stranded well outside the fledgling "safety net" of the time.

Most people in Uncle C.'s situation became "shut-ins"—housebound and isolated. The Lewis family, though, was determined to have Uncle C. avoid that fate. He couldn't go to school, so his brothers and sisters took turns teaching him in the evening what they had learned during the day. To get him around, my father and his brothers scrounged neighborhood scrap piles, salvaging wheels from a junked pram and enough lumber and nails to build my uncle a cart.

FREDA LEWIS-HALL

1960: The Lewis nieces and nephews visit Uncle C.
as he recovers from spinal fusion as a result of his
polio. I'm the angelic-looking girl on the far right.

They put Uncle C. in the cart and took him wherever they went.
That was one of my father's earliest memories—the Lewis boys walking down the street or heading off to the sandlot, with their brother
always in tow. My father later said that while he thought he and his
brothers were "pulling Uncle C. along," Uncle C. was actually "pulling them along"—teaching them to rise to society's challenges, and be
compassionate and understanding.

This story turned out to be more than just a heartwarming family
memory. With the confidence he gained from the Lewis brand of main-
streaming, Uncle C. became a tailor, and a good one. He designed and
made clothes for me and taught me how to sew. He also gave me my

first paying job. At age three, I was "employed" by my uncle to snip the ends of the threads as he sat working his sewing machine. I still remember the thrill of achievement when he would slip a few pennies into my palm.

Uncle C. earned his way and eventually became a teacher in the Prince Georges County, Maryland, school system, teaching his trade to others who were disabled. By the time he died in 1995, he had taught hundreds of seriously disadvantaged students the fine trade of tailoring.

Uncle C.'s story speaks to legacy and to leadership. From him, I learned much about succeeding in a resource-starved world, the dignity of honest work, the power of learning, the strength of the human spirit, and the ultimate power of loyalty and love.

I also saw, first hand, the "multiplier effect" of energy invested by leaders in helping others make progress. In bringing Uncle C. behind, both literally and figuratively, my father and his family opened the doors of opportunity for hundreds of youngsters they would never meet. What was thought to be a kids' project—a cart built from discarded wheels and scrap wood—ended up bringing productive careers to some of the most seriously disabled children of Prince Georges County.

Five Dollars Can Change the World

I experienced a stirring example of conscious thinking about the "multiplier effect" when I heard the president of Morgan State University, Dr. David Wilson, talk about the events that shaped his life. David is only the twelfth president of this historically black university, which was founded just after the Civil War, and is located not far from where I grew up in Maryland. He has produced an amazing body of work over an illustrious career that included stints at Tuskegee, Rutgers, Auburn, Wisconsin and Harvard—institutions that must have seemed so far away when he was working the fields alongside his father, an Alabama sharecropper.

Dr. David Wilson, the president of Morgan State University, applies the lessons learned from his father, a sharecropper, to improve the futures of disadvantaged students.

MORGAN STATE UNIVERSITY

David grew up in scarcely imaginable deprivation. He and his siblings had to take turns going to school, so that the crops could be raised and brought in on time. Much as my father and his family did for Uncle C., in David's family, any child who was given the "day off" to attend school taught the others at night and kept them honest on their homework. David was a good student and began to think about college even as he was breaking his back harvesting vegetables. Working in the fields one day, he spoke about college to his father, who responded tersely: "College is for white folks." They never spoke about it again.

Five years later, David announced to his family that he had been accepted at Tuskegee University. There was no response from his father. Then, at daybreak one September morning, just before David set off for his first day of college, his father called him aside. He said that he had put away every bit of money he could for David's education, and in fact had started saving when David first mentioned college as they worked side-by-side in the fields.

The rugged sharecropper reached into his pocket and pressed all his savings into David's hands. It was five dollars.

Since coming to Morgan State, David has set aside a substantial portion of his salary to fund scholarships for students who might be shut out of college over a tuition gap of a few hundred dollars. These scholarships don't come for free—with them comes the expectation that they will be paid forward, as well as the demand that the students engage, listen to, and learn from a diligent mentor.

The Joys and Responsibilities of Mentorship

As people around me know, I'm a firm believer in the power of mentoring. I've benefited immensely from diligent mentors, and tried to be one to dozens of people during my career.

There isn't a standard formula for successful mentorship, nor is there a secret to it. Mentor relationships are hard work. "Who you bring along" takes serious time and thought. The ones who do it best pour their hearts and souls into it. One of the best is Jim Robinson III, the former head of American Express and the current Presiding Director of Coca-Cola. Jim's legendary reputation for networking is anchored in a disarmingly simple approach. He makes sure that those he mentors become integrated into his vast network. Sounds simple, but it's not easy. It takes time, discipline and energy on all sides of the relationship. At its core, "Who you bring behind" should remind us that at some point, our roles as leaders will end and we must be ready to give way to the leaders we have indeed "brought behind." As we have seen time and again, the reluctance to prepare a new generation of leaders and then step aside for them can inflict considerable damage on even the most successful and well-established organizations.

"Honest Mentorship"

When people ask me for advice on bringing along the next generation of leaders, I start with the most essential word in human relations today: honesty. It's the thread binding the responsibilities of coaching, evaluating, mentoring and sponsoring.

I started thinking through the concept of **honest mentorship** after sitting through session after session by trainers encouraging us, as leaders, to be "brutally honest" in counseling those we serve as leaders or mentors. I subsequently thought about the numerous performance management systems I have worked with during my 35-year professional career, and, to be direct, started comparing the typical output of these systems to the simple approach espoused by my parents: to be *both* my most honest critic *and* my biggest cheerleader.

Honest mentorship includes both **compassionate honesty** and **honest praise**. The first concept, compassionate honesty, addresses two of the most common roadblocks to leadership development: **resistance** and **insensitivity**. It's an enormous challenge for leaders to invest the time needed to provide useful counsel to "leaders in training." It always takes time and is often uncomfortable. As a result, many "leaders in training" don't learn about their shortcomings, weaknesses or blind spots until their careers are close to derailing or have already gone off the tracks.

My mentor Alice F. Oliver told me that the reluctance by leaders and followers to address shortcomings in an honest fashion makes those weaknesses bigger than they should be, and their eventual (and nearly inevitable) revelation can seriously damage the psyche of the follower. It's a sad fact of corporate life that many people dismissed by organizations for unacceptable performance previously had long records of solid or even exemplary performance. At some point something dramatic happened. Too often, it was the squaring-up of a performance appraisal with the person's actual performance.

The opposite of compassionate honesty is "brutal honesty" and the first word says it all. How often do we mistake obnoxious or controlling leader behavior during the coaching process for the "brutal" in brutal honesty? And how often do important messages go unheard or unheeded by the overwhelmed, often-hurt recipients of poorly articulated counsel?

Compassionate honesty makes it clear that providing insufficient counsel in even the most amiable fashion is as counterproductive as providing sufficient counsel in harsh or hurtful ways. It's time to transform the empty exercise that too often passes for performance management into a productive experience with compassionate honesty—an abundance of clear, cogent advice, rooted in dignity and respect for the individual.

I was exposed to compassionate honesty early in life. My mother had an innate ability to both bring out the best in me and to help me see where I could improve. She took every opportunity to reinforce me when I did well and to speak up, constructively but directly, when change was needed.

In addition to compassionate honesty, it's time for a return to **honest praise**. Leaders who are highly proficient in bringing other people behind them certainly provide lots of coaching, in sensitive and highly caring ways. They also give sincere praise when it is warranted, anchoring that praise in behaviors and outcomes that the leader wants in his or her follower. One of the best at this is Charlie Sanders, the former chairman and CEO of Glaxo, Inc. (now GlaxoSmithKline), and current chairman of the Foundation for the National Institutes of Health—FNIH.

Charlie is a true "Renaissance Person" whose list of achievements includes leading one of the nation's most important medical centers, Massachusetts General, running for the U.S. Senate, and serving as a medical school professor at Harvard. Now in his 80s, he chairs the FNIH with vision and energy but also goes the extra mile to serve as a mentor to many of the younger scientists doing high-risk medical research. He knows what it's like to invest a large part of a career in biomedical research, and understands the mindset of a committed scientist.

Charlie has an uncanny ability to hone in quickly on a person's strengths and he often has matched those he mentored with projects well-suited to those strengths. He helps his mentees build a "base of success"—guiding them through important projects and praising them for jobs well done, especially during the early stages of the mentorship relationship. There are few feelings more gratifying than receiving Charlie's praise in front of your peers. You can be confident that it's praise well earned, but it also helps you feel that you can accomplish anything. And that's how Charlie wants you to feel—because it means he's getting ready to ratchet up the "degree of difficulty" in the work to be done!

I've learned from many mentors, starting with my parents all the way through Charlie Sanders, that praise is essential as long as it's warranted. Providing honest praise for people who perform consistently at high levels is to me the hallmark of an effective leader.

Models of Honest Mentorship

When I look for models of honest mentorship, I turn to three of my most crucial mentors—my mother, Jeanette Lewis; my teacher at Howard University Medical College, Dr. LaSalle D. Leffall, Jr.; and a colleague at Lilly, the late Dr. August "Gus" Watanabe. None of them was my "manager" in the sense that organizations now use that word. Each took vastly different approaches to the concept of "who you bring behind." All three were models for the brand of honest mentorship I espouse.

Jeanette Lewis—Mommy and Mentor

My mother, Jeanette Lewis, set the tone. I was an only child and not exactly the life of the party. I was a bookworm and seen by my peers as somewhat odd. While my friends were chasing after baseball cards and Barbie clothes, I collected mice and snakes, which I liked to carry around in my purse. (Note: not at the same time.) My idea of a big day out was visiting the National Museum of Health and Medicine outside Washington, D.C.—with the first stop being the arcade of human organs preserved in formaldehyde.

And I wondered why no one liked me.

One afternoon I came home very upset and, after a bit, asked my mother to help me understand why I wasn't liked. I didn't get it—I was a good person, I worked hard and helped people. I cried my heart out and then, after most of my tears had dried, my wise mother and mentor turned the question to me.

"If you are who you think you are, why don't your friends see it? And what can you do about it?"

"Maybe," I said, **"I need to work to turn them around."**

Then my mother cut to the heart of the problem, answering softly, **"Perhaps, but maybe you need to work to turn *you* around."**

From there, she led me to explore how we could "turn me around" and present a new image to my friends—an image that was authentic but also more readily accepted. So I kept my pets but stopped pulling field mice out of my purse and wearing a snake around my neck. (Let's call that the "low-hanging fruit" of the turnaround process.)

The lessons I learned from this compassionately honest exchange were "shape-shifting" in my life. On the receiving end of mentorship, I learned to pay much more attention to those around me and to listen more intently for cues that my approach wasn't in sync with everyone else's. On the giving end of mentorship, I learned the value of on-going honest feedback, with appropriate enthusiasm for each moment of accomplishment, large and small. I also learned the value of direct, timely feedback as an opportunity to discover and develop yourself.

Dr. LaSalle D. Leffall, Jr.— No Nonsense, But Plenty of Passion for People

People around the world revere Dr. LaSalle D. Leffall, Jr., and for good reason. Now in his 80s, Dr. Leffall was, for nearly six decades, one of the nation's preeminent surgeons and he remains one of our most honored medical educators. Every day, thousands of doctors in leading medical centers around the world put to use the lessons Dr. Leffall taught them. He's the embodiment of the "multiplier effect"—the

HOWARD UNIVERSITY

One of the nation's most
brilliant surgeons and
storied medical educators,
Dr. Leffall's chance meeting
with me in a hallway at
Howard University ended
up changing my life.

leader whose abilities to lead, inspire, teach, and serve drive many
others to aspire to and reach similar heights.

In Dr. Leffall's case, those heights were pretty lofty. He graduated
from a segregated high school in Florida at age 15, shortly before
the end of World War II. Accepted to Florida A&M, he obtained his
bachelor's degree with highest honors in just three years and went on
to Howard University College of Medicine, where he graduated first
in his class. He then became one of the youngest physicians ever li-
censed in the United States.

As a new doctor and aspiring surgeon, Dr. Leffall faced his own trials
in a largely segregated society. He was the third African-American to
become a surgical oncology fellow at what is now known as Memorial
Sloan-Kettering Cancer Center in New York City. While in training
there, he became certified by the American Board of Surgery. In the
late 1950s, he served his obligatory military service and achieved another milestone, becoming chief of general surgery at the Army's huge

hospital in Munich, Germany. From there, he joined Howard's faculty and is now the first holder of one of the university's most prestigious endowed chairs in surgery: the Charles R. Drew Chair.

Dr. Leffall's skill in surgical oncology was the stuff of legend. If someone had to open your gut and cut out a cancer, you wanted it to be Dr. LaSalle D. Leffall, Jr. When President Ronald Reagan had serious surgery on his colon in July 1985, Dr. Leffall was tapped by *CBS Evening News* to serve as an on-air expert and explain the president's surgery and prognosis in plain language to the American people. It was among the first times a network newscast featured an African-American doctor as an expert in science or medicine.

A Willing Mentor

At Howard, Dr. Leffall was more than a living legend. He was an active mentor to a number of medical students, including me. He had the quality of compassionate honesty, but that didn't mean he was going to let the unprepared go unchallenged. A meeting with Dr. Leffall wasn't something you took lightly. If he asked you to consider a question, you came back with well-formed answers. He never said it, but he made it clear that mentorship shouldn't be confused with friendship. His time was his most precious resource; he gave it generously but expected it to be used well.

My first year at medical school was difficult, as it is for many students, with thousands of pages of readings and hundreds of hours in the anatomy labs. A few weeks into the maelstrom, my then-boyfriend and future husband, Randy, phoned me from Philadelphia where he was in law school. He had distressing news. Doctors had found a suspicious mass during a routine physical exam. He was headed for immediate exploratory surgery. During the surgery, his mother and I sat in the waiting area. She was pacing and smoking. I was doing my best to study, but mostly I was crying. The surgeon came in to tell us what we both somehow knew. Randy had cancer. "Randy is young and otherwise healthy, so his prognosis should be good," said the surgeon, but he tempered his optimism with a warning: "There's a long, hard road ahead."

We soon found ourselves in for a terrible ride. My constant worry and frequent trips from Washington to Philadelphia made keeping up with medical studies almost impossible. The emotional roller-coaster ride was nearly unbearable. I wanted to take a "break" from med school to be by Randy's side. My mother, though, strongly encouraged me to stick with school, and I did. My first year in medical school ended on an optimistic note. Randy was on the mend, and I had scraped through "hell-year."

Just as I thought I had survived the earthquake, the aftershocks hit. My beloved mother suffered a massive stroke one warm summer night and died within days. The suddenness of her death, the challenges of helping my family get her affairs in order, and the responsibilities of caring for my grieving, Alzheimer's-stricken grandmother drained me. I returned to Howard after the summer break more exhausted than when I had left.

Dr. Leffall and I had numerous discussions after I returned to keep me centered on my medical training. One day, though, I decided I just couldn't take it anymore. I convinced myself to take a leave of absence and then come back strong the following year, knowing full well that nearly everyone who voluntarily stops their medical education never returns to it. I believed I would be the exception.

Most of my classmates were heading to class that morning as I was walking in the opposite direction, on my way to the Dean's office to ask for my leave. I ran headlong into Dr. Leffall, who saw me swimming against the tide of humanity, and called out, "Aren't you going the wrong way, Dr. Lewis?"

That's all it took for me to open up and let him know of my plans. He listened. He agreed that the pressures were immense and that I was still in the throes of grief. Then he started to walk, beckoning me to come with him. He let me know that he believed in my great promise as a healer. He reminded me that becoming a doctor was my lifelong dream. He asked if I thought that leaving medical school was what my mother would have wanted. All the while, we walked and, as he finished his last thought, we found ourselves at the door of the lecture hall. He then turned on his heels and left, never looking back. He knew I was going back into class—and I did.

Dr. Leffall has touched the lives of thousands of physicians and millions of patients and caregivers. I'm very fortunate to be among this lucky multitude.

Dr. August "Gus" Watanabe: The Go-To Guy

My third "model of mentorship" is Dr. August "Gus" Watanabe, who was the long-time head of research for Eli Lilly—my first stop in the biopharmaceutical industry after working for nearly a decade as a doctor, teacher and medical researcher.

The son of a chicken farmer, Dr. Watanabe was a research dynamo widely credited with helping Lilly find its way forward after a string of patent losses. The company launched nearly a dozen new products

CHARLIE NYE/THE INDIANAPOLIS STAR

Dr. August "Gus" Watanabe, the longtime head of R&D for Eli Lilly. His mentorship helped me make a challenging transition from academia to corporate life.

under his R&D leadership. Even today, Lilly benefits from projects that he helped initiate.

I don't know why—perhaps because we both made the leap from academia to the pharmaceutical industry—but Dr. Watanabe took special interest in me from my first day at Lilly back in 1994. I came to the company with almost no idea about how to operate effectively inside a huge corporation. Strange acronyms and terminology flew by me at meetings. It was often "inside baseball" and I felt like the kid stuck in left field.

Dr. Watanabe and I spoke often and our conversations were incredibly helpful as I made the transition to corporate life. One of my biggest challenges, an issue that is still tough for many of us in the medical field operating in business environments, was learning the perspectives of my business colleagues. I wanted to know what they knew and to speak their language. I also wanted them to understand that I was part of the team.

But these conversations weren't always smooth, as there were sometimes genuine differences of opinion. Sometimes I wanted it both ways—to be seen as the protector of the patient, and to please my colleagues in the marketing department. After one difficult meeting, Dr. Watanabe pulled me aside and said, "Dr. Lewis-Hall, we hired you to be a medical leader. Not a marketing leader. Not a brand leader. So just be the doctor you took the oath to be. Your job is to bring the patient into the room, as only you can do. You do that right, and the team will make the right choices."

That's advice I continue to hear from, and give to, members of my division at Pfizer and to all those in the medical community broadly. The patient must always come first. Do that, and the right decisions will follow.

Who You Bring Behind

"Who you bring behind" is my favorite element of legacy. To paraphrase what was once said about the Peace Corps—developing the next generation of leaders is the hardest job you'll ever love. As a leader of people, a coach, a mentor, a sponsor, and/or counselor, you have the opportunity to create your own "multiplier effect"—and watch it change lives and build futures.

For this to happen, however, you need to answer several key questions as honestly as possible. How are you bringing the next generation behind you? How much are you investing in the people who can help bring you behind? How much time and effort are you devoting to developing the people who will lead tomorrow, however you define leadership, and wherever leadership is needed in society? And what are you doing for yourself?

Chapter 4

What You Learn
Along the Way

My father's third and final "pressure test" of legacy speaks to what we learn along the way in our careers and our leadership experiences. Of course, learning by itself is of little use unless we apply what we have learned to what we do. Learning forms an endless "virtuous cycle" in life. The more you learn and apply those learnings, the better leader you become.

Mel Goodes, the corporate executive whose story appears in this chapter, put it best when he was leading a fast-growth, Fortune 100 company in the 1990s. "The day I stop learning is the day that the board should fire me," he said. "Everyone should learn something new each day on the job. Learning should be just as important to a CEO as it is to a person fresh out of college."

My life has been filled by lessons I've learned from people who have overcome enormous challenges to succeed. Here are a few of them.

Your Burdens Are Your Blessings,
Your Blessings Are Your Burdens

Starting with "burdens," my friend Alice F. Oliver freely admits that her childhood was miserable, but goes on to say that meeting the challenges of her early life paved the way for her to overcome ever-greater obstacles during her career, and even in her family life. This included a parent's worst nightmare, the death of a child. The full sum of her life's burdens, she says, showed her that she had the strength to push through the deepest valley of her life.

At the same time, we all know people who are immensely blessed with talent, skill and even charisma. But then something happens. They achieve a certain level of success only to derail because of some element in their personality that was once positive but is now holding them back. My friend Marshall Goldsmith, one of the world's most prominent (and commonsense) coaches of high-level executive leaders, makes precisely that point in his book, "What Got You Here Won't Get You There," a critical excerpt of which is quoted, with his blessing, below:

> **"Successful people believe in their own success. But these beliefs also carry the seed of our failures: the beliefs that carried us here—which can be a pretty great place—will impair our ability to progress there—which can be performance at the next level."**

I learned that "blessings can be burdens" the hard way, and fortunately, with some mentoring, kept myself from derailing early on. When I was a medical school professor at Howard University, I became intensely interested in healthcare disparities, particularly among minorities and women. I was invited to deliver some lectures on this topic and to serve as a special advisor to the Director of the National Institute of Mental Health.

At the time I was in my early 30s, and at the peak of sassiness. And frankly, a measure of "sass"—a kind of "take no prisoners" approach to getting the job done—was a highly praised trait during my early career. I loved going over to the NIH—me, a young, female, African-American psychiatrist and acknowledged expert—and lecturing older doctors on the truth of the world, from my point of view. That I couldn't find any good data on anxiety disorders in African-Americans, well, that was their fault. The huge mental health disparities rooted in race, income or location—well, that too was their fault. I never hesitated to point out what I believed was their fault.

I began to wonder why I got so little cooperation from the doctors on projects that the NIH itself had proposed. And why empty seats soon outnumbered attendees at my lectures.

Eventually I was summoned to the office of Dr. Delores Parron, then the associate director for Special Populations of the National Institute of Mental Health. Dr. Parron had been a mentor since my days in medical school, and a role model for thousands of women like me. She was a scientist at heart. Encouraged in scientific studies by a Catholic nun at Georgian Court University, where she was the only African-American student in her class, she launched her distinguished career in science in 1966, about the same time I was hauling mice around in my purse. She went on to teach at Howard and earned her doctorate in behavioral sciences from Catholic University in 1977, when she was recruited to the Carter Administration. Dr. Parron became an ardent voice for closing the gap in healthcare disparities and helped craft the legislation that created the Office of Special Populations in the National Institute of Mental Health to assure increased emphasis on the mental health needs of women and minorities. She was also the first person to lead that office, and for her, failure in that position was not an option. When she spoke, people listened—including me.

She was the epitome of gravitas when I arrived at her office. Sitting behind her desk, arms folded, she greeted me with, "Sit down, young lady" and nodded towards a waiting chair. I was in for what my mother would call "a good talking-to."

"If you want to get through to your colleagues here, leave your sass in the parking lot and get yourself under control," she said.

I argued that I was just being authentic, just being "me"—and just being honest, brutally honest. She waved that argument away. "Well, if being 'authentic' is a code word for being obnoxious, good luck with that," she said. "I know the authentic you, and this is not it. Bring the best of Freda—now that would be authentic!"

At that moment, I heard, and yes, learned, two powerful lessons.

First, that being "authentic" didn't mean bringing *all* of me *all* of the time. I could be strong in convictions and principles, and be authentic without being abrasive. I wanted my legacy to be a person who brought out the best in others, and not someone best avoided in the hallways.

I also learned that compassionate honesty has a place not only in mentoring but also in daily dealings with collaborators, colleagues, and even antagonists to your cause.

Throughout my career, I've witnessed the serious derailment of top leaders, all too often because they couldn't leave their "sass" in the parking lot, or understand how to stand strong on their convictions without alienating those around them. The common themes of these derailed leaders is an overreliance on past successes and a reluctance to adapt to life and leadership on a larger stage. The blessings—the traits that forged a leader's success in the past—often become the burdens that eventually sink his or her career.

"If Something Is Out of Reach, Move Closer"

I've mentioned Uncle C. and his struggles with polio. Life was not easy for him. Every day, he confronted the difficulty of something placed out of his reach. He fashioned tools to extend his reach and bring things to him. Figuratively as well—Uncle C. always found that extra "oomph" inside him to move closer to something just outside his grasp. His headstone is inscribed with what he said so often to us—"If something is out of reach, move closer."

How often do we want something that is clearly out of our reach but refuse to take the first steps to getting closer, even if those steps don't always carry us all the way to our goal? And how much power could we have if we would just "move ourselves closer"?

In 2011, I made a business trip to India, my first extended visit to that dynamic and fascinating nation. I had the good fortune to meet there with several leading thinkers who are applying leapfrog strategies to India's brand of healthcare. One of them was Dr. Devi Prasad Shetty, the chair of cardiac surgery for Bangalore's Narayana

Hrudayalaya Hospital and one of the founders of that hospital chain. The hospital's vision is a marvel of inspirational simplicity: "affordable quality healthcare for the masses worldwide." Turning that vision into a legacy may mean that billions of people will have access to levels of healthcare once available only in highly developed economies.

Trained in both the U.K. and India, Dr. Shetty is today one of India's most prominent surgeons. His patients included Mother Teresa, the nun who worked with the poorest of the poor in Kolkata. After watching him treat a child with a severe heart defect, Mother Teresa told him that she knew why he was put on earth—to relieve the agony of children. She also shared with him one of her most famous sayings, one that brings both surgeons and tailors to mind: "Hands that sew are holier than lips that pray."

Dr. Shetty's blessing as a skilled surgeon comes with a self-imposed burden—to put the benefits of advanced surgery into the reach of the average citizen of India. The problem with this goal is pretty clear: best-in-class approaches to neonatal, pediatric and adult cardiac surgery are also the most expensive. Complex cases run easily more than $100,000, clearly out of reach of all but the richest or best insured people in the world. Even the lower labor costs in India cannot entirely close the gap between what the vast majority of the world's people can afford and what a hospital must charge to sustain its operations.

How could Dr. Shetty make advanced surgery more accessible to people of modest means?

He began a relentless drive to attack the cost of hospital care, but from a different angle. Rather than organize the hospital to attract the rich and then extend itself to treat the poor as charity cases, Dr. Shetty designed the hospital to serve the poor as its primary customers and then find ways to attract the rich. Increasingly, these richer patients are coming from wealthier nations where people either cannot afford complex cardiac surgery or find their options restricted by national reimbursement programs. In addition, the hospital, in partnership with India's government, launched micro-insurance programs to reach millions of rural families and embrace them in a modest healthcare safety net.

When it came to wringing out costs, nothing escaped Dr. Shetty's scalpel. Whole hospital wings were designed from the ground up for speedy service and infection control. Dr. Shetty and his team re-engineered the entire intake-to-discharge process, and, where necessary, hired support staff to free surgeons from paperwork. The goal: have surgeons do what they do best—surgery, leaving other activities to experts at those tasks.

In an interview with FastCompany magazine, Dr. Shetty noted that, "More than 100 years after the first heart surgery, less than 10 percent of the world's population can afford it." He's out to vastly expand that percentage and, in doing so, move the world closer to a place where all people have access to even the most complex lifesaving surgery.

Be Ready to Speak Up

At the risk of sounding like the psychiatrist I was trained to be, I am convinced that the internal restrictions we put on ourselves in speaking up about problems in the workplace are, at best, self-limiting and, at worst, self-defeating. In my own case, I know it's hard to speak up, to honor my real voice and make my opinion known. As "out there" as I am, I still have the little voice in my head that often tells me to keep quiet and not rock the boat. Sometimes I just have to gag that little voice and shove it aside.

The reluctance to speak up often has painful personal consequences, from failed relationships to derailed careers. Victoria Medvec, a professor at Northwestern University's Kellogg School of Management, and Executive Director of its Kellogg Center for Executive Women, believes there's a link between the lack of women in leadership positions and the reluctance of women to be bold and speak up. Women, she says, are often hesitant to negotiate for themselves and are reluctant to ask for opportunities and projects as well

KRISTA KENNELL/FORTUNE

Victoria Medvec helps women develop their negotiation skills and prepares them for senior leadership positions in the corporate world.

as promotions. She also notes that women are conditioned to be averse to risk, which can impede them from taking on profit-and-loss responsibilities in a company. "P&L" experience is generally the track to general management and senior leadership in the corporate world.

Consequently, Victoria invests much of the work of the Center for Executive Women on helping women assert their rights to ask questions and negotiate for themselves. One of her goals is to equip more women at a younger age with strong negotiation skills, to stave off self-defeating behaviors before women reach middle management.

During his acceptance speech for the 2012 HBA Honorable Mentor Award, Michael Kaufmann, the CEO of Cardinal Health's pharmaceutical segment, noted the difference between men and women in pursuing a new career opportunity. "If there were six hiring criteria for an open position," he said, "most women would wait until they had all six before they applied for the job. Men, on the other hand, if they had one ..." He did not need to finish. The women in the ballroom understood the point, many of them from first-hand experience. We all need to speak up as our own best advocates and to take action, not wait for it.

Demonstrate 'Equanimity Under Duress'

I've talked about how Dr. LaSalle D. Leffall, Jr., the retired chief of surgery at Howard University College of Medicine, became one of my most important mentors. He had a mixture of composure, confidence and calm that was his trademark approach to leadership, which he termed "equanimity under duress."

Dr. Leffall's approach was forged in the crucible of his life—the challenges he faced and overcame in his education, in his service to our nation, and in the first decades of his surgical practice. He overcame outright discrimination and much more by force of will and confidence in his talent as a surgeon. He instilled confidence in others by radiating confidence, a sense that things were under control or could be brought under control.

This approach to leadership is absolutely essential in the surgical suite. Needless to say, a patient being prepared for surgery wants to know that the surgeon wielding the scalpel is fully prepared, centered, and committed to the success of the task at hand. Inside the surgical suite, the patient is under anesthesia while the surgical specialists work. The pace is rapid, the unexpected can arise at any time, and decisions have to be made quickly and communicated with precision. "Equanimity under duress" is important in the success of the operation, because anything less jeopardizes the patient.

"Equanimity under duress," though, extends to all kinds of leadership situations and is the cornerstone of many leaders' legacies. It is a quality of leaders who understand their responsibilities but who are also open to options and alternatives—and are respectful of the talents of the people around them. Leaders demonstrating "equanimity under duress" take into account ideas from all sources, then make decisions mindful that others are looking up to them at critical moments for direction and inspiration.

One of the most compact and complete lessons in "equanimity under duress" can be found in three minutes of conversation that took place in the skies over New York City on January 15, 2009. The dialogue was led by the captain of a US Airways' Flight 1549, Chesley Sullenberger, and included the air traffic controller responsible for his flight, and a variety of other aviation specialists in the New York metropolitan area.

The story is well known. Just after taking off from LaGuardia airport in an Airbus A320 bound for Charlotte, N.C., Captain Sullenberger and his crew ran into a flock of geese that knocked out the jet's two engines. In an eyeblink, Captain Sullenberger—"Sully" as he is known—was back to a brand of dead-stick flying he had not done since the Air Force Academy.

One of the most telling elements of these cockpit recordings is the way everyone went about their business calmly, with composure, and with all due speed. It's hard to believe that the most radical of solutions, landing in the Hudson River, was being discussed as if it is just another day at the office. Captain Sullenberger was firmly in charge of the chain of information and ready to make decisions based on the best options open to him or seen by others. The storybook ending is that he made a water landing without the loss of any lives aboard. He executed the entire stressful sequence with equanimity, from his first reports on the bird strike to his last actions as the captain of the ship—walking through the thigh-deep water onboard the just-ditched plane and making sure no passenger had been left behind.

In contrast to the minute-by-minute emergency situation faced by Captain Sullenberger, "equanimity under duress" can also be seen in leaders dealing with more long-term, highly stressful situations. Such is the story of Dr. Hawa Abdi, known widely as "Mama Hawa."

Dr. Abdi, one of Somalia's first gynecologists, lives and works on a stretch of land outside Mogadishu—land owned by her family for generations. She established a small but effective women's clinic on the land in 1983 to serve Somali women. When the government collapsed several years later and warlords carved up Mogadishu, her patients flocked to her for safety—first a trickle, then a deluge. Currently, the camp has more than 90,000 refugees, living in relative peace but suffering from constant threats of violence and a precarious supply of food and water. Those seeking refuge include men and women who have endured atrocities nearly beyond belief.

With her daughters, Mama Hawa has managed to keep her refugee enclave going despite attacks by militiamen. With heroic composure

PIETER HUGO/DHAF

Somalia's Dr. Hawa Abdi, known to millions of people as "Mama Hawa," established a safe haven that is now home to thousands of refugees displaced by violence.
I was honored to meet Mama Hawa and was personally moved and inspired by her composure and compassion.

and strength—the ultimate in "equanimity under duress"—Mama Hawa continues to stand up as a force for peace and goodwill in a desperate corner of the world.

Hope Is the Currency of Leadership

Whether through the calm reserve of Captain Sullenberger or the heroic stance of Mama Hawa, the call for hope is a common thread in leaders. If, as the Rev. Martin Luther King, Jr., once said "Everything that is done in the world is done by hope," then every leader in the world deals in the currency of hope.

As leaders, we parlay hope into action. We work to sustain hope as long as there is even a modest chance of success. What leaders are expected to do and do often—the legacy they leave—is to keep hope alive. As Rev. King put it, leaders "accept finite disappointment but never lose infinite hope."

My parents taught me hope by continually telling me that I could do anything I set my sights and heart on. When I was a child, age six, and decided to become a doctor, they were ready and willing to help me keep that hope alive, even when it appeared, at times, that my dream might die.

One story of hope concerns Mel Goodes, whom I introduced to you at the outset of this chapter. Mel is the retired chairman and CEO of Warner-Lambert, a pharmaceutical and personal care products company purchased by Pfizer in 2000. Mel was born in 1935 at a time when hope was mighty scarce. He grew up in the steel town of Hamilton, Ontario, when the Depression decimated the steel business. Mel's father left school at age 12 to go to work, and Mel almost did the same, but instead, at his parents' urging, became the first in his family to graduate from high school.

He went on to Queen's University in Kingston, Ontario, and from there to the University of Chicago as a Ford Fellow. His professors included George Shultz, who would later serve as Secretary of the Treasury and State, and Nobel Prize-winning economist Milton Friedman.

After a short stint at Ford, Mel joined Warner-Lambert. He was a country manager at age 30 and running a major consumer products segment a few years later. In the mid-1980s he became chief operating officer and then in 1991 took over as chairman and CEO. He jokes that he got the job because "they couldn't find another sucker to take it." Warner-Lambert, in serious decline, and dogged by patent expirations and manufacturing woes, was being described by analysts as among the "walking dead of the pharmaceutical industry."

Mel had one last card to play, a lipid-lowering compound in development called atorvastatin. The strict business case for atorvastatin was not compelling, but Mel made a leap of faith and authorized a clinical trial. Its results were promising and eventually it was approved by the FDA. The drug became Lipitor, Warner-Lambert found a partner to co-promote it in Pfizer and the rest is history. Pfizer ultimately bought Warner-Lambert and Lipitor became one of the world's most important medicines. In 1999, Mel retired, having guided Warner-Lambert back to prominence during his time at the helm.

Following the Alzheimer's disease diagnosis of retired Warner-Lambert CEO Mel Goodes, he and his wife, Nancy, have become a powerful team advocating for greater investment in Alzheimer's research.

ROB RICH/SOCIETYALLURE.COM

As notable as these achievements are, it is Mel's "second coming," as he calls it, which may be his most important legacy. In 2010, Mel and his wife, Nancy, were stunned by a doctor's diagnosis that Mel had early-stage Alzheimer's.

It would have been easy for Mel and Nancy just to pack up and enjoy the remainder of their time in the cognitive world for Mel. But they couldn't do that. Mel believed it was now his role to offer some measure of hope to others. He and Nancy became involved with the Alzheimer's Drug Discovery Foundation (ADDF), a not-for-profit organization that was launched by the Lauder family. ADDF provides funds for promising compounds that are having trouble attracting investment in this time of shrinking R&D budgets.

On top of that, Mel offered to begin discussing his diagnosis in public to demystify Alzheimer's and give it a face. Particularly striking, he spoke of the first months after his diagnosis, when the full effect of an Alzheimer's prognosis began to sink in.

"Remembering all the times I faced long odds and didn't blink, I wondered: 'Why can't I beat Alzheimer's, too?'

"Then, over a few days, the reality sets in: Alzheimer's disease is pitching a perfect game. No matter how hard you swing, you are going to be out."

Mel said he and Nancy now had a vision for the rest of their lives. They would be advocates for ADDF and for Alzheimer's patients and caregivers everywhere. Alzheimer's may win in the end, he said, but he sure wasn't going gently into that ragged night.

Today, still an active volunteer for Alzheimer's research, he talks of his first speech two years ago, and his reference to the "perfect game" being pitched by the disease.

"Alzheimer's might still be pitching a perfect game but it's now been two years, and I am still at bat. I'm still swinging for the fences."

AMERICAN ASSOCIATION OF
PHYSICIANS OF INDIAN ORIGIN

"Your vision should never let you rest." So says
Dr. A. P. J. Abdul Kalam, former president of India,
whom I was honored to meet in 2011.

The hope that Mel and Nancy inspire in patients, caregivers, physicians, and researchers demonstrates what General Colin Powell said hope is—a "force multiplier."

It's important to sustain hope in your vision and your leadership. Sell hope—real hope, not false hope—to those you lead. It's your best chance to rally others to help you achieve your driving vision, the vision that as Dr. A. P. J. Abdul Kalam, former president of India, most elegantly put it, should never let you rest.

Chapter 5

Make Your Mark!

I started this book with a discussion of the past. Let me end it with some thoughts on our shared future.

But first, back to the past.

Despite the three "pressure tests" for legacy that my father laid out for me, I continued, as a teen, to obsess about my own legacy. I kept pestering my parents about the concept to the point where they finally sat me down, put their hands on my shoulders and told me, "Honey, if you want to leave a legacy, start by leaving a mark. **Your marks will become your legacy."**

The Need for I-doers

Like most parental pronouncements, this one makes a lot more sense now than it did then. In the space of a modest book, I can only address some of the many people who left positive, affirming marks on me. But they all shared a common mindset. They didn't leave these marks by accident or by happenstance. They knew the importance of what they were doing, and how their "collection of marks" would someday comprise their legacies. They knew that they were called to leadership in a way that would not only produce followers but also new leaders. Whatever their status in life, they were conscious and thoughtful about how they made their marks on me and so many others. It was never "about them." It was always "for us."

That ideal, "for us," can have significant, enduring and positive consequences for our world. In healthcare and in many other arenas, we see the "multiplier effect" of the marks made by people who are far from the upper echelons of an organization, but who understand that they can profoundly change their corner of the world. As my husband Randy puts it, **"I appreciate ideas, but I need I-doers."** The greatest ideas in the world lie fallow without the I-doers of the world—people willing to move themselves, and others, toward the idea.

The Power of Our Marks

As I travel around the world, I see people from all walks of life making their marks, but often underestimating the power of their actions. Many times a person's "mark" comes disguised as something else—such as making a living.

In 2010, I went to Africa with my colleague, Sally Susman, who leads Pfizer's initiatives in communications, public affairs and social responsibility. Our goal was to assess the progress of several partnerships in which Pfizer is playing a key role. Among them is the International Trachoma Initiative (ITI), a partnership founded in 1998 by Pfizer and the Edna McConnell Clark Foundation.

ITI's "no-rest" vision is to eliminate blinding trachoma, one of the world's oldest recorded diseases and one that is almost entirely preventable. Caused by a variant of chlamydia, trachoma still affects up to 70 million people, with nearly 5 million of them facing imminent danger of blindness. ITI's leadership believes the partnership can wipe out blinding trachoma by 2020—a vision that is, in corporate parlance, "ambitious but achievable."

Sally and I visited a number of villages where we saw both the immense pain of trachoma and the equally immense possibilities of finally wiping this tragic disease off the face of the earth through a combination of better hygiene, surgical intervention and medicine.

During the Africa trip, I knew that there was a lot of ceremony accorded us and the government officials sharing our visit, but I also knew that when we had packed up and gone home, the collaborative team efforts would continue, with ITI workers quietly but effectively making their marks, whether that be coordinating surgery, arranging lessons on hygiene, ensuring people get and take their medicine, or providing clean drinking water. These are totally unheralded leaders who are changing the course of a disease, one village at a time.

In 2010, in Ethiopia's Amhara State, I observe Dr. Tebebe Y. Berhan administer Zithromax®, the antibiotic needed to help prevent blinding trachoma. Along with me are my colleague Sally Susman, Sid Scruggs, President of the Lions Club International Foundation, and Dr. John B. Hardman, CEO and President of The Carter Center. Public-private partnerships such as the International Trachoma Initiative hold the potential to transform access to healthcare and roll back the tide of infectious, treatable diseases.

Inspired by my experience in Africa, I recently accepted an offer to join the board of trustees for Save the Children. Their funding approach is very well known: individuals offer a monthly donation and get personally connected with a child who is benefiting from Save the Children programs. What's usually not recognized is the "multiplier effect" of these and other modest donations. Anne Mulcahy, the highly successful, now-retired head of Xerox who leads the Save the Children board, told me that the collective effects of these "marks"—the reliable modest donations over a number of years—are transformative for needy families around the world.

The power of our marks is also demonstrated in the stories my father told me about his life as a Pullman porter, taking care of passengers in the luxury railcars of the immediate post-war era. Pullman porters were all male and all black, serving exclusively white and generally well-heeled customers. For many travelers, a trip by luxury overnight train was the first time they came face-to-face with an African-American for any period of time. That reality wasn't lost on the porters.

Overnight trains became rolling classrooms of the civil rights movement. Pullman porters often endured a barrage of humiliation in order to demonstrate, one passenger at a time, that they were fully equal members of the human family. It is little wonder that many of the leaders of the civil rights movement spent time as Pullman porters. They learned a great deal about collective intent and persuasion, and they understood the power they had to "make their mark."

Leadership gives us the chance to amplify our influence, but we should never forget that change occurs one person at a time. I remember the first time I found myself standing in a place to amplify my influence beyond the walls of Howard University. It was in 1989, when I had the opportunity to do a healthcare talk show on a local PBS affiliate in Washington, D.C. As discussions progressed, I met with Ed Jones, the station's general manager, and we talked about the premiere of my show, *The Urban Health Report*, and its first segment, focusing on diabetes.

"Freda," Ed asked, "what do you want to get out of this?"

I told him something to the effect that I wanted to reach the people of the world, and bring them better healthcare through better information.

Ed looked at me and said, "Uh-huh … try again."

"I want the people of Washington and …" Ed stopped my thought short by shaking his head.

I stammered, "Okay, okay. I want one person—one—who didn't know he or she has diabetes to find out because of the show. I want to save those legs, those eyes, those kidneys, that heart because of one thing we do in the half-hour we're on the air!"

Ed said, "Dr. Lewis-Hall, *that* we may be able to do."

About three weeks later, I was in the supermarket near my home in Washington, and saw an older gentleman coming down the aisle. He looked at me, I looked at him. He smiled, I smiled. Finally he said, "Ain't you that young child on television?"

I liked the "young" part. "Yes, sir, I am."

He continued. "My daughter was watching that show and says, 'Daddy, come here. You need to do this.' And so we go off to the doctor and sure enough, I had a touch of sugar [diabetes]."

Then he hugged me. **Here he was, my one person I wanted to touch.** I had made my mark.

Today, I appear on TV shows reaching millions, including the daytime health program, *The Doctors*, on CBS. I take my guest appearances on this show and others with dead seriousness and with great awe for the power of the camera. We plot our on-air time word for word, second by second. Whatever I am saying, however I am saying it, I want people to think about their families and say to themselves and to their loved ones "We need to do this."

Gathering Our Marks—
Collective Intent and Metacollaboration

When I was a kid, I used to (surprise!) obsess about the times I had to talk in front of the class. I'd practice in front of a hastily drafted audience usually consisting of my aunts and uncles. Eventually, my Uncle Big Daddy would give me a hug and tell me not to leave my best performance on the rehearsal stage. "Remember, Sugar," he'd say, "If you can't be profound, be provocative."

I don't know if my ending to this book will be profound, provocative, neither or both. But here goes.

I love to laugh, to joke, to have fun with my family and friends. Having seen life from some of its most difficult vantage points, I can put many facets of my work-a-day world into perspective, including the balance of work and family.

I take the concepts of leadership and legacy very seriously. I understand the importance of making marks, and know that all of the people in this book, and thousands of others I could never hope to list, made their marks on me. They showed me that leadership—and legacy—aren't about ego or self-indulgence. Genuine leadership, in fact, is quite the opposite. It's a serious matter, because the consequences of *not* having effective leadership can be dire.

If any human endeavor cries out for more leadership, it's healthcare. I thought about that a lot on the spring day in 2011 when I took the podium at HBA's "Woman of the Year" luncheon and spoke from the heart about my 30-plus years as a doctor, researcher and healthcare leader.

I've devoted my entire life to healthcare and, until now, have never seen it engender such a wide range of emotions, from elation over diseases conquered to despair over the reality that 40 million Americans and 4 billion of the world's people are stranded without the healthcare they need.

I meet with scientists almost daily who are genuinely thrilled about their work. They are peering into the origins of disease at the molecular level and designing medicines that may someday plug disease pathways or zap cancer cells with laser-like precision. Their excitement is palpable, and rightly so. Then I look at the realities of healthcare innovation, and the model of innovation we have now, and know that only a small number of the thousands of scientists devoting their lives to biomedical research will ever be associated with a new medicine or vaccine.

All of us fret over the harsh realities of healthcare—the struggle to improve research productivity, the booming cost of treatment, the tragedy of people dying way too soon from diseases for which there are, or should be, ample treatments. We keep hearing about "tipping points" for the research-based drug industry, for healthcare insurers, for governments. Meanwhile, obesity, diabetes, arthritis and Alzheimer's disease are all approaching their tipping points as well.

What is the way forward? How do we keep patients from being on the wrong end of a host of "tipping points"?

I don't have all the answers, but I believe that we, as healthcare professionals, have to find our way forward by "turning us around," to quote my mother. We have to stop thinking that the problems of healthcare lie with someone else and see that, as the comic strip character Pogo put it, "We have met the enemy, and he is us."

I am convinced that behind the power of **collective intent**, and with metacollaborations—collaborations an order of magnitude above what we have now—we can walk ourselves back off the ledge and sustain and expand access to healthcare.

Now, I'm realistic about the limits of healthcare access. We can't provide perfect care to everyone. But can't we at least close the gaps in healthcare access to the point where we can look ourselves in the eye, knowing that there aren't children in the world dying for lack of ten-dollar mosquito nets? Can't we get people to understand that they need to know as much about their blood chemistry as they know about celebrity chefs or storage locker bidding wars? Can't we, as a society, have a meaningful dialogue about aging without pitting one generation against another?

This is going to take leadership at all levels. It will take new, radical ideas, maybe even whole new business models. More to the point, it's going to take a generation of "I-doers"—people dedicated to the reality that the patterns of the present are just not sustainable, not if we believe that advanced healthcare is for more than just a small group of wealthy people or nations.

The question, "Which way forward?" extends far beyond healthcare. Nearly all of our essential systems seem to be in crisis. Whatever the proposed solution, it's always "them" that need to get "turned around."

Maybe it's time for us to first turn ourselves around and then, together, turn the world around.

I don't mean this lightly and I don't bring it up to end on a "down" note. I am a firm believer in the power of collective intent, and an even firmer believer in the power of leaders at all levels to catalyze that collective intent.

I am old enough to remember when U.S. cities were torched by racial strife, when a president came on the airwaves to warn the nation of the possibility of superpower nuclear war, and when scientists wondered if HIV/AIDS would consume the world before it could be controlled. In each case, the situation got "turned around" because of leadership at *all* levels, and from *all* corners; because everyone from the president to the person washing the lab floor went forward to make a mark.

Our Time Is Now

The timing for a broader vision of leadership could not be better. If there is a silver lining in the erosion of trust in the traditional leadership of our society, it is that trust has migrated to, literally, "people like us."

Early in 2012, Edelman released its annual survey of trust, and the results, while never great, were even worse than usual. The number of nations where people generally trust their major institutions is receding faster than the polar ice caps. The only bright spots in trust were for "typical employees" of an organization—and for "people like us."

We have seen the future, and it will be shaped by "people like us." The world is now putting more of its trust in people who may not be at the very top of organizations but who in fact have the collective power to change things.

It is clear that a future marked by trust in leadership can't be determined by a small group of people making decisions for others. It *can* be shaped by groups of leaders open to new forms of collaboration, new levels of collective intent, and a renewed commitment to an age-old concept—that leadership has to be taken seriously by leaders if *they* expect to be taken seriously by followers.

If people are now looking to you for leadership, how will you respond?

Will you take the mantle of leadership seriously?

Will you recognize how critical it is to make your marks?

Will you pass my father's three "pressure tests" of legacy?

As I stood on that platform at the HBA luncheon in 2011, looking out over the thousands of leaders present, I couldn't help but sense the energy in the room, the excitement about the new generation of leaders coming to the fore, and the confidence in our collective will to master the world's most serious challenges.

I could not help but think of my Uncle C.'s words, and one of my life lessons—"If something is outside your grasp, move closer."

The call to "move closer" is upon us. Legacy still counts, and it counts for a lot. Shaping a legacy depends on your heart, your will, your commitment. You can begin the process of change today—now! In doing so, you can build a body of work to be proud of and profoundly change a corner of the world—and leave behind, for years to come, a network of the inspired.

FREDA LEWIS-HALL

Family Portrait, 2005. My family is the guidestar of my life.
My husband and heartthrob, Randy Hall, continually reminds
me, "People don't change when they see the light. They change
when they feel the heat." I am optimistic that the "heat" of
the world's healthcare situation will drive us to collective
and unprecedented positive action, building a healthier
world for our children and the generations behind them.

About the Author

Freda Lewis-Hall, M.D.

Industry leader, medical researcher, teacher, mentor, doctor, caregiver, patient advocate and former talk show host Freda Lewis-Hall, M.D., has invested more than four decades in exploring both human health and the human condition. Currently Executive Vice President and Chief Medical Officer for Pfizer Inc., Freda began her career as a practicing psychiatrist in the Virgin Islands and then "made her mark" as an expert in examining the deficiencies in care accorded women and minorities. Moving to the corporate world, she's held senior leadership positions in companies such as Eli Lilly, Bristol-Myers Squibb and Vertex Pharmaceuticals before coming to Pfizer in 2009, where she is the company's top physician.

In 2011, Freda was named "Woman of the Year" by the Healthcare Businesswomen's Association, one of the world's largest professional societies serving those at the nexus of business and healthcare. **Make Your Mark! Why Legacy Still Matters** is adapted from her "Woman of the Year" acceptance address.

A regular guest on daytime TV shows such as *The Doctors* and *Rachael Ray*, Freda can be found at www.pfizer.com/health/cmo.

About the Healthcare Businesswomen's Association

The HBA is one of the world's most prominent professional associations devoted to healthcare. Its membership of more than 6,000 women and men includes leaders from biotech, healthcare products, managed care companies and pharmaceutical manufacturers as well as leaders from publishing, advertising, medical education, communications, and other service providers. HBA members share a strong commitment to helping each other advance and look to the HBA for opportunities to work with and to get to know professionals at all levels throughout the industry. The HBA empowers members as they develop and hone their personal leadership agenda, knowledge and skills. Association involvement helps members remain at the cutting edge of market trends and create a network of contacts that are instrumental in achieving career goals.

HBA sponsors a number of outstanding leadership programs, including the Leadership in Practice series—a strong online program tailored to the needs and resources of leaders in the middle-to-upper levels of organizational leadership.

If you want a boost on learning how you can bring people behind, take a look at the leadership programs sponsored by the HBA. They have online and in-person programs tailored to the needs of leaders in the middle to upper levels of corporate management. Visit www.HBAnet.org for a full listing.